WRITING IS MY THERAPY

A Collection of Self-Love Inspiring Prompts to Overcome Trauma

Marissa F. Cohen

Dedication

This book is dedicated to the millions of amazing survivors of narcissism, abuse and assault in the world who are doing their best to overcome. You are strong and brave. But you're not alone. And this journey you're on is easier and quicker with the help of others. So, let people in. We are here to help you live a Free, Confident and Peaceful life.

Dear NCCC Wellness Center:
  Cheri, Hannah & Ericka,
Thank you so much for having me at NCCC! Your students are amazing and I'm honored to be your DV & SA speaker! I look forward to collaborating with you again!

Sincerely,

Marina F. C

Be Free,
Confident and At Peace!

If you put a frog in a pot boiling water, it'll jump right out. But if you put a frog in a pot of luke-warm water, and gradually turn up the heat, the frog will acclimate and then burn to death.

Abuse doesn't start off horrible and aggressive, or else we would just leave. It starts of slow, and boundaries are pushed, until it becomes explosive and dangerous.

We experience a lot of deception and confusion, and it teaches us to be more weary of the people around us. But know this, there are people you can trust. There are survivors all around you that can relate to what you went through, and can be an amazing inspiration and support system for you. You have a TEAM around you, willing to be there when you need us, and to help guide you through your healing journey.

You are worthy. You are loved. You are smart. You are capable. You are enough.

Your experience doesn't define you. What you do next to overcome your narcissism and abuse, does.

— Marissa F. Cohen
Founder of the Healing From Emotional Abuse Philosophy ™
Best Selling Author of the Breaking Through the Silence series
www.MarissaFayeCohen.com

If you, or someone you know is struggling to overcome the aftermath of abuse/assault, please reach out for help.

Schedule a FREE 30 Minute Session with Marissa F. Cohen and get the support you need from someone who understands.

www.ScheduleACallWithMarissa.com

You are not alone!

Write About Your Favorite Memory.

Write a letter to yourself from yourself now,
when you were in your darkest day. Give
yourself encouragement,
because you made it out alive.

Have you talked about your trauma?
Why or why not?

Identify 25 things/people you're grateful for.

_____
_____
_____
_____
_____
_____
_____
_____
_____
_____
_____
_____
_____
_____
_____
_____
_____
_____
_____
_____
_____
_____
_____
_____
_____
_____
_____
_____
_____
_____
_____
_____
_____
_____

I Am...

(Pick 3 words to describe yourself. Ex: Strong, Brave and Kind)

_____,

_____,

& _____!

*Write a letter to the person who hurt you the
most. Tell them everything you've been
holding in, and don't hold back.*

*Make a list of your coping mechanisms and
how they have worked for you.
Positive and negative.*

_____
_____
_____
_____
_____
_____
_____
_____
_____
_____
_____
_____
_____
_____
_____
_____
_____
_____
_____
_____
_____
_____
_____
_____
_____
_____
_____
_____
_____
_____
_____
_____
_____
_____
_____
_____

Describe the life you want to live with as much detail as you want.
What does it feel like to be living that life?

Take yourself on a walk. Appreciate all the nature around you, and let your mind wander.

Tell yourself something that you need to hear.

_____
_____
_____
_____
_____
_____
_____
_____
_____
_____
_____
_____
_____
_____
_____
_____
_____
_____
_____
_____
_____
_____
_____
_____
_____
_____
_____
_____
_____
_____
_____
_____
_____
_____

Write a letter to your best friend and tell them how much you appreciate them in your life.

What do you feel about your day today? Why?

What made you feel happy today?

What made you feel stressed today?

When I think of myself, I feel...

Describe your dream partner. What do they look like, act like, feel like, etc.?

_____
_____
_____
_____
_____
_____
_____
_____
_____
_____
_____
_____
_____
_____
_____
_____
_____
_____
_____
_____
_____
_____
_____
_____
_____
_____
_____
_____
_____
_____
_____
_____
_____
_____
_____
_____
_____
_____

Give yourself a Pep-Talk in the mirror, as if you were talking to your best friend.

What do you need to hear today?

What makes you feel safe?

Make a list of songs that make you feel empowered? Then turn it into a playlist.

Write about a memory that bothers you.
Something that you can't get out of your head.
Write everything about it, and release it.

Today is going to be a good day, and here's why...

_____
_____
_____
_____
_____
_____
_____
_____
_____
_____

What do you envy about someone else and why?

Describe yourself in 5 words and explain them.

Make an Acrostic Poem using the letters of
your name and explain them.
Ex. M- Magnificent, A-Articulate, R- Respectful, I.... etc.

_____
_____
_____
_____
_____
_____
_____
_____
_____
_____
_____
_____
_____
_____
_____
_____
_____
_____
_____
_____
_____
_____
_____
_____
_____
_____
_____
_____
_____
_____
_____
_____
_____
_____
_____
_____
_____
_____

Where is your dream vacation and why?

Write a bucket list of 100 things you want to do, see or have.

_____
_____
_____
_____
_____
_____
_____
_____
_____
_____
_____
_____
_____
_____
_____
_____
_____
_____
_____
_____
_____
_____
_____
_____
_____
_____
_____
_____
_____
_____
_____
_____
_____
_____
_____
_____
_____
_____

"Life is not about waiting for the storm to pass, it's about learning to dance in the rain."

Write about a scary moment for you. What was happening? How did you resolve it?

What about yourself do you hope to change?

What are some patterns you've noticed in your life? How can you change them?

_____
_____
_____
_____
_____
_____
_____
_____
_____
_____
_____
_____
_____
_____
_____
_____
_____
_____
_____
_____
_____
_____
_____
_____
_____
_____
_____
_____
_____
_____
_____
_____

List 3 things you love about yourself and explain why.

_____

_____

_____

_____

_____

_____

_____

_____

_____

_____

_____

_____

_____

_____

_____

_____

_____

_____

_____

_____

_____

_____

_____

_____

_____

_____

_____

_____

_____

_____

_____

_____

Set yourself a boundary, and be willing to stand by it.

What about yourself are you proud of?

On the spokes of this wheel, write all the people and things in your life you're grateful for.

What have you learned about yourself in the past year?

What are 5 goals you want to accomplish in your lifetime?

_____
_____
_____
_____
_____
_____
_____
_____
_____
_____
_____
_____
_____
_____
_____
_____
_____
_____
_____
_____
_____
_____
_____
_____
_____
_____
_____
_____
_____
_____
_____
_____

Write 3 affirmations that mean something to you, and then draw them.

Affirmation #1

Affirmation #2

Affirmation #3

What is one thing you can do today that will make you feel empowered and happy?

_____
_____
_____
_____
_____
_____
_____
_____

Describe a day that started out bad but turned out good.

Think about the things you say to yourself —
the negative self-talk. Write them, and then
rephrase them as strengths.

"What you want exists.
Don't settle until you
get it!"

-Jay Setty

Write down 5 activities/exercises that make you happy. Why do they make you happy?

*What are your triggers that cause you to be
anxious? How can you avoid them?*

Write about a time that you had a positive
interaction with someone and it changed your life.

What makes you feel the most confident?

Who is someone in your life that always seems positive? How can you learn from them and develop a more positive mindset?

_____
_____
_____
_____
_____
_____
_____
_____
_____
_____
_____
_____
_____
_____
_____
_____
_____
_____
_____
_____
_____
_____
_____
_____
_____
_____
_____
_____
_____
_____

Who are you the most positive around? Who brings out the happiness in you?

_____
_____
_____
_____
_____
_____
_____
_____
_____
_____
_____
_____
_____
_____
_____
_____
_____
_____
_____
_____
_____
_____
_____
_____
_____
_____
_____
_____
_____
_____
_____
_____
_____

Who are you the most negative around? Who makes you feel bad or grumpy?

_____
_____
_____
_____
_____
_____
_____
_____
_____
_____
_____
_____
_____
_____
_____
_____
_____
_____
_____
_____
_____
_____
_____
_____
_____
_____
_____
_____
_____
_____
_____
_____
_____
_____

Do you express feelings easily?
Why or why not?

When was the last time you cried, and what helped you feel better?

What is your love language? How can you provide yourself with this kind of love?

Write 3 things that inspire you to be your best self.

Three things I'm good at are...

1. _____
2. _____
3. _____

Why do you think you struggle with self love?

Make a vision board.

1. Pick words, pictures, and phrases that inspire you.

2. Paste them to a poster board.

3. Hang that poster board next to your bed so you can see it every morning when you wake up, and every night before you fall asleep

What makes you feel loved?

How do you think your life would change if you accepted and loved yourself as you are today?

_____
_____
_____
_____
_____
_____
_____
_____
_____
_____
_____
_____
_____
_____
_____
_____
_____
_____
_____
_____
_____
_____
_____
_____
_____
_____
_____
_____
_____
_____
_____
_____
_____
_____
_____
_____

When was the last time you were proud of yourself?

_____

_____

_____

_____

_____

_____

_____

_____

_____

_____

_____

_____

_____

_____

_____

_____

_____

_____

_____

_____

_____

_____

_____

_____

_____

_____

_____

_____

_____

_____

_____

_____

Describe a time in your life when you felt the most confident.

_____
_____
_____
_____
_____
_____
_____
_____
_____
_____
_____
_____
_____
_____
_____
_____
_____
_____
_____
_____
_____
_____
_____
_____
_____
_____
_____
_____
_____
_____
_____
_____
_____
_____

Who are the 5 people in your life that you feel you can really rely on?

_____
_____
_____
_____
_____
_____
_____
_____
_____
_____
_____
_____
_____
_____
_____
_____

Who are the 5 people in your life that you are most grateful for and why?

_____
_____
_____
_____
_____
_____
_____
_____
_____
_____
_____
_____
_____
_____
_____
_____
_____
_____
_____
_____
_____
_____
_____
_____
_____
_____
_____
_____
_____
_____
_____
_____
_____
_____

Be the person for others that you needed in your darkest moments.

What are three things you would tell your past self?

_____
_____
_____
_____
_____
_____
_____
_____
_____
_____
_____
_____
_____
_____
_____
_____
_____
_____
_____
_____
_____
_____
_____
_____
_____
_____
_____
_____
_____
_____
_____
_____
_____
_____
_____
_____

What are 3 things you'd tell your future self?

What are 5 things you want to remind yourself when you have anxiety?

_____
_____
_____
_____
_____
_____
_____
_____
_____
_____
_____
_____
_____
_____
_____
_____
_____
_____
_____
_____
_____
_____
_____
_____
_____
_____
_____
_____
_____
_____
_____
_____
_____
_____

If you could travel anywhere in the world,
where would you go and what would you do?

Write a letter to someone who had a negative impact on your life.

Write an encouraging letter to read to yourself on a bad day.

Make a list of the people in your life who you
love, trust and respect.

_____

_____
_____
_____
_____
_____
_____
_____
_____
_____
_____
_____
_____
_____
_____
_____
_____
_____
_____
_____
_____
_____
_____
_____
_____
_____
_____
_____
_____
_____
_____
_____
_____
_____
_____
_____
_____
_____

Where do you see yourself in 3 years?

Turn your
CAN'Ts into CANs
and your
DREAMS into PLANS!

Write a letter to yourself today from you in 5 years. Talk about where you are and how you got there.

Write about the day you felt the most free.

Healing Coach & Corporate Trainer

Breaking Through the Silence Together

Thank you for supporting the voices of survivors, speaking their truth and Breaking Through their Silence. The first step to healing is sharing your story and speaking out about your trauma. And it's important to know that you are sharing with a supportive person or community. There is nothing more empowering than facing your trauma with people who have been there holding your hand and validating how you're feeling.

The Breaking Through the Silence series has been awarded by Readers Favorite, Amazon, and survivors everywhere, praising the exceptional contribution these books have made for survivors. If you have a story that you would like to contribute to future books in the series, to help other survivors feel heard and validated, we would love to hear it.

The Breaking Through the Silence team is committed to protecting survivors identities. The last thing we want is to make anybody feel in danger or targeted. So, for that reason, we change any identifiable information for every survivor, to protect their anonymity and confidentiality. It's important to me that all of the survivors that choose to participate feel completely empowered, but also secure and safe. These books are meant to spread awareness to support. So, we do whatever we need to, to make you feel absolutely comfortable.

Below are 4 questions about your story. Answer them with as much or as little information as you're comfortable with. You are in control of your story. We are grateful you're choosing to participate.

There is also future book topics for the BTTS series. Check off any and all that you feel your story applies to.

And finally, there is an interview release form attached to this document. In order for us to use your story, we need you to read and sign the interview release. And as a "Thank You" for participating in BTTS's attempt to change the perception of sexual abuse and domestic violence in society, it will be my pleasure to send you a copy of the BTTS book(s) that you participate in.

Please either write your responses on this document and send it back and send it back using the envelope provided; or email them directly to **Marissa.Faye.Cohen@gmail.com** with "BTTS CONTRIBUTION [Your Name & Topic]" in the SUBJECT line. You can send them in written form or voice recordings. Whichever method is easier and more comfortable for you.

Topics:

- ☐ Military
- ☐ LGBTQIA+
- ☐ Wrestling Speaking Out
- ☐ People With Disabilities

- ☐ Reported But Nothing Happened
- ☐ People of Color
- ☐ Intimate Partner Violence / Spousal Abuse

- ☐ Child Abuse
- ☐ Stalking
- ☐ Violent Crimes
- ☐ Workplace
- ☐ Other: _____

Questions:

Question 1: Please, tell me your story, with as much or as little detail as you're comfortable.   Include any aftermath you felt or faced. Write it as if you're talking to a friend.

_____
_____
_____
_____
_____
_____
_____
_____
_____
_____
_____
_____
_____
_____
_____
_____
_____
_____
_____
_____

Question 2: What resources have you used to help you heal? They can be positive or negative (drugs, alcohol, self harm, therapy, coaching, writing, music, activities, etc.). What worked? What didn't work?

_____
_____
_____
_____
_____
_____
_____
_____

_____
_____
_____
_____
_____
_____
_____
_____
_____
_____

Question 3: What changes need to be made in society, the judicial system, or any support outlet to make overcoming abuse and assault easier for survivors?

_____
_____
_____
_____
_____
_____
_____
_____
_____
_____
_____
_____
_____
_____
_____

Question 4: What advice would you give to survivors to support their healing?

_____
_____
_____
_____
_____
_____
_____
_____
_____
_____
_____
_____
_____
_____